CW01502178

$\mathscr{I}$LLUSTRATIONS

THE SOLDIER

THE SOLDIER

by

Tony Thomas

The Pentland Press Ltd
Edinburgh · Cambridge · Durham · USA

© Tony Thomas 1998

First published in 1998 by
The Pentland Press Ltd.
1 Hutton Close
South Church
Bishop Auckland
Durham

All rights reserved.
Unauthorised duplication
contravenes existing laws.

British Library Cataloguing in Publication Data.
A catalogue record for this book is available
from the British Library.

ISBN 1 85821 591 9

Typeset by George Wishart & Associates, Whitley Bay.
Printed and bound by Antony Rowe Ltd., Chippenham.

$\mathcal{F}$OREWORD
by
Lieutenant General Sir Rupert Smith KCB DSO OBE QGM

It gives me the greatest pleasure to write a Foreword to this enjoyable book.

To me, a young and inexperienced officer, Tony was a constant source of wise council and practical advice. As you will read, he had seen it all before: from big wars to little fights, from Arnhem to Aldershot, and from prison to Palace. His deep understanding of his fellow men, and in particular the soldier, was obvious in all he did, and set an example for us to emulate. No doubt he had to work harder on me, for, as he explains, those of us in 3 Para were always a bit backward in Tony's eyes.

I commend this book. It tells the story of one of the nation's 'centurions' whose enduring courage, dedication, decency and good humour shine out of every page.

CHAPTER I

In July 1921 I made an inauspicious entry into a world recovering from the mindless slaughter and devastation of the First World War. There was much unemployment, especially in the North-East where I was born. I was the middle of three brothers and four sisters, and my father worked for ICI in Billingham as a block-maker, producing cement blocks.

Our house was in Summerhouse Square, Norton-on-Tees near Stockton and part of it was a shop at the front, which my mother ran as a sweet shop. Unfortunately she was later forced to close it as there was high unemployment in the area and people could not afford even the cheapest of luxuries.

As children, my brothers and I played outside in the street a lot and as I was never very tall, I was forced to learn how to look after myself in the many scrapes and street fights which we were involved in. Although football was our favourite sport, I also found out the hard way how to defend myself often in scraps with boys bigger than myself which must have been very useful when I took up boxing more seriously in my teens.

Living in and around Stockton, the local accent was – and is – true 'Geordie', not the gutteral sound of the people of Newcastle and Gateshead, but the one found in the country areas of north Durham and Northumberland. Jack Charlton, brother of Bobby, is a prime example of one who speaks true 'Geordie'. My family was Catholic and so I went to the local Catholic-run Junior School. When my maternal grandmother died, she left her house in Vicarage Avenue, Stockton to my mother, and the family moved there in the early 1930s. At about that time I moved on to the local Catholic Secondary Modern school, St Bede's; my best friend was Tooker Jordinson. With him and my younger brother I often used to go camping in the summer by the River Tees near Yarm-on-Tees, either on foot or by bike, and we would climb trees and swim in the river.

I remember that there were a lot of suicides, as it was the later years of the depression, and unemployed people with no hope – both men and women – would commit suicide by drowning themselves in the River Tees. The local councils would pay for the recovery of any body from the river – 5/- per body on the Durham side and 7/6d on the Yorkshire side of the river. We as boys would recover a body floating in the river and drag it ashore or to the wharfside, making sure it was on the Yorkshire side! One of us would then fetch the local police, while the others guarded the body, so that we could claim the reward, which was sent to us in the post by the local County Council in the form of a postal order. Unbeknown to me at the time, I was to see many dead bodies during the War, so I suppose my early introduction to handling the corpses of those poor unfortunates on the banks of the River Tees was to prove useful later on.

As a boy I was known as 'Twicey' which I hated. This came about because my surname was Thomas and my christian name was also Thomas. When I was confirmed, I had my christian name changed to Anthony and insisted that I was called 'Tony' – which I have been known as ever since.

There was one incident which I can recall, when I was about fourteen. We used to go into the market in Stockton to watch and listen to the traders. There was one called Jack Cowie who sold a soap which he claimed would cure anything from dandruff to piles. I remember making a cheeky remark about his product for which I received a cuff around the ear from him. Looking round I saw a car with a length of rope looped round its bumper, so I took one end of the rope and tied it to the leg of his stall without him seeing. Minutes later Jack was in the middle of his sales patter when the driver of the car got in and drove off, bringing down the canopy of the stall and covering Jack in a cascade of soap tablets. I stood there laughing so much and for so long that I was arrested by the police and was taken before the local magistrates, who severely reprimanded me and put me on probation for two years.

I liked being at school as I enjoyed the company of others, and was sad when it was time to leave. By then I had matriculated in several subjects, the best of which were English and History. My two older brothers, meanwhile, had found it impossible to get work near to home and so both had gone to London to seek their fortunes. They stayed initially in lodgings and Griff got a job as a storeman, while Bob became a car salesman.

I had no ambition to do anything in particular with my life, but my first job was with the Co-op Butchers, Yarm Lane, Stockton where the manager was a very pleasant man called Tom Mason. I was employed initially as a butcher's boy, delivering meat by bike to local residents and businesses. Later I was moved to the abattoir where I learnt how to butcher or 'chine' carcasses. Cattle were slaughtered by humane killer, and sheep and pigs with electrodes. My salary was about 12/- per week which went into the family kitty. I worked there for about two years and although I could have stayed on and been promoted within the abattoir I decided to move on. War clouds were gathering on the horizon, and so I opted to join the Army.

CHAPTER II

I had been in gangs and fights throughout my childhood, and had always liked the sound of the Army even though there was no obvious military presence in Stockton. There were no barracks or military displays, and the nearest recruiting office was in Middlesborough, but I had had enough of the abattoir and the spectre of unemployment was not a pleasant one – I'd fished too many bodies out of the River Tees!

So I decided to give the Army a go and signed on as a Supplementary Reservist – younger men under the age of seventeen who could not be posted abroad – for seven years with the colours and five with the reserves. It was July 1938 when I joined the Durham Light Infantry (DLI) and started my six-months' recruit training in Fenham Barracks, Newcastle-upon-Tyne. It was a totally new world.

I was woken on my first morning by the urgent notes of reveille ringing out from the square below, and lay there listening to the chorus of farts and Woodbine coughs from the other young would-be soldiers around me, struggling to come to terms with their new lives.

We had in our barrack room an old Geordie soldier (OS)

called Cushy Butterfield who had twelve or more years' service. To us he was the fount of all knowledge, although we were later to find out that he was called 'The know-all that knows bugger-all'. As an old soldier he was there to help us recruits and answer our many questions, however, when I got out of bed on that first morning and went over to ask him innocently what we should do, he just said, 'Bugger off!' – a great help, but I did as he smelt like a dead camel. We soon discovered that he had an overactive bowel and you could smell him at ten paces, but in time we learnt all the secrets from him.

Getting back into my strange bed on that first morning away from home I tried to doze, but was promptly disturbed again by a spitting, snarling monster of a man who came into the barrack room, poked us all with a stick – which we were later told was a pace stick – and ordered us to get out of bed, wash and shave. Or words to that effect! We were informed by Cushy that he was the Platoon Sergeant Major (PSM), which was a new rank introduced by Mr Hoar Belisha. We were to get to know him well during our recruit training and were soon able to distinguish some English in his snarling. He wore a crown on his sleeve without the wreath, and his pace stick was an extension of his arm. I asked Cushy if he was human or something out of Sedgefield – the local lunatic asylum, apart from now being the Parliamentary seat of Tony Blair – but was given my first lesson in the Army and was told to listen and disseminate.

We were to learn a lot from Cushy in those six months of recruit training. We used to sit round the barrack room stove to be regaled by his exaggerated stories which I am sure he made up as he went along, but he had a wonderful accent and we would all listen spellbound until lights out. He told us he was educated, but we discovered later that all he had was his Army Third Class Certificate of Education which meant he could just about read and write. He said he could speak three languages, but when I, like a fool, asked him which ones he replied, 'English, Urdu and Obscene!'

He was an old Indian hand and his speech was peppered with bastard Urdu, which I, too, was to learn when I joined the Battalion. To close the door was to 'bunkeraro the wazy', while phrases like 'ek dom' (straight away), 'tyro' and 'tora' (wait a moment) were commonplace.

The food was only mediocre and we had porridge ('bergoo') every morning without fail. Our pay was 1/6d per day, so between the Naafi and outside the barracks, we did not have a lot to spend. You could 'barter' a pair of army socks at the Naafi for a supper meal as the Naafi would then sell the same grey army socks to another soldier. We had sheets and four blankets on our beds, and every morning we had to 'box' the blankets and show one item of kit. Cushy would tell the PSM when he knew of any individual who was missing a particular item of kit – and sure enough, that would be the one that had to be shown in the morning. In that way he would drop us in it, but it taught us to look after our possessions.

After several weeks we were allowed to 'walk out' of the barracks in uniform, including cut-away trousers and long puttees. Before going out through the gates, we were inspected by the the Provost Sergeant or one of his staff, and

Early days wearing Service Dress adapted from the First World War with white General Service belts. The PSM and Corporal are wearing 1908 pattern belts. Dark green backing on DLI collar dogs. Author is centre of rear row.

if our turnout was not up to standard we were not allowed out.

Towards the end of my recruit training I started going to the gym twice a week, after training had finished for the day, for my first boxing lessons with Sergeant Sampson, an old boxer in the Army Physical Training Corps (APTC). I already knew how to look after myself in a scrap, and so it did not take long for me to pick up the finer points of boxing and how to move around the ring. Soon I was good enough to appear in a local boxing booth, Blacks Regal Circuit.

I would leave the barracks with my boxing strip on under my uniform and go to the fairs on the town moor in the hopes that I would have a bout because on a good night you could pick up £5 or more. If the crowd thought you had put up a good show, win or lose, they would throw coins – or 'nobins' – into the ring when the fight was over. Naturally the seconds kept most of these, but it was a good feeling to be earning such good money thanks to the Army. You would never know your opponents until you met in the ring – I took some beatings, but I had my share of wins, some by knockout and others on points. The referees on the whole were fair and it was they who judged the winner.

In those days you could go out on the town with a tanner (sixpence), have a pint and a packet of Woodbines, go to the pictures up in the gods for twopence, and still have a fish and chip supper on the way back to barracks. We would walk down from Oxford Galleries to the Monument to see if there were any girls about – or 'bints' as Cushy called them. The word in the ablutions in the morning would be that there could not have been a virgin within a mile of Fenham Barracks.

My recruit training finished in January 1939, just eight months before the start of the War. I do not remember any passing out parade as such, but I was then posted to the 2nd Battalion DLI which was stationed in Inkerman Barracks, Woking in Surrey.

CHAPTER III

The 2nd Battalion was busy training for war, but it seemed that the lessons of the First World War had not been learnt, and I was very surprised by the number of mounted officers in the Battalion. The only form of wheeled transport in a rifle company was the horse-drawn kitchen, and when a company went on a route march it would be split into platoons, with the company commander leading on horseback, and the kitchen wagon at the back with the cook walking beside it stirring the food!

The Battalion was almost 1,000 strong, and I can well remember being under canvas on Chobham Ridges with the Household Cavalry. We would dig trenches and defend them against the cavalry, who would charge over us as we cowered at the bottom – a very unnerving experience!

Only sergeants and above were allowed to have their families with them in those days, so there were not many of them and the married quarters were strictly out of bounds.

Having sat and passed my Army Certificate of Education, Third Class as a recruit, I went back to 'school' again and got my Second Class Certificate as well which I needed before going on a junior NCOs' cadre. Having passed that too I was promoted to lance corporal – but lost my stripe two months later when I and some friends 'borrowed' a car one night to get back to barracks. When we were all questioned later about the incident I owned up to the theft, was reduced to the ranks and given fourteen days detention in the Military Corrective Training Centre (MCTC) in Aldershot. One morning there I was down on my knees whitewashing a flight of steps when one of the guards, or 'screws', deliberately walked down the steps, all over my handiwork. When he reached the bottom I lashed out at him – and was given another seven days! You never walked or marched anywhere at the MCTC – everything was done at the double, but this didn't bother me as I was from a Light Infantry battalion and was used to marching at 140 paces to the minute with rifle at the trail.

After my stay in the 'glasshouse', I returned to the Battalion a wiser man, where I got back to real soldiering again on the local training areas, and regained my stripe by the end of the year. But by now war had been declared, the Battalion was about to be moved across to France and so I became a member of the rear party in Woking as I was still too young to be posted abroad. The RQMS was in charge of this party, which consisted of a small 'Q' staff and a dozen or so of us Supplementary Reservists, plus a couple of NCOs to look after our training.

Whilst in Woking I was able to keep up my boxing training, and on Saturdays would take the regimental bus, or 'passion wagon', up to the Union Jack Club in Waterloo Road, London, go by tube to Blackfriars where there was a big boxing centre and, as a featherweight, take part in bouts, often as a replacement for someone who was injured or had not turned up. I used to be paid the enormous sum of £20 which was a lot of money in those days and considerably boosted my meagre army pay at the time of 2/- a day! Although as an amateur I was not allowed in the ring with a professional, one Saturday I was matched against one from South Africa – and beat him! He was later charged with murdering his girlfriend by pushing her out of a porthole on board ship.

Sadly my lucrative boxing career was interrupted when I was posted at the end of 1941 to the DLI's training depot at Brancepeth Castle between Durham and Willington, which was a small mining village. The depot was the training centre for all recruits joining the DLI, which at that time had six battalions, to be increased to sixteen by the end of the War. But while the camp was being built, there was insufficient barrack accommodation for us and so we were billetted in the village of Willington. We took over the village hall and miners' recreation centre to house the recruits, and used the streets of the village as a drill square.There was a sergeant and a couple of junior NCOs for each recruit squad – I was a drill and weapon training instructor.

There were six platoons in each recruit company and the NCO instructors stayed with the same squad of recruits throughout their two months' basic training. In addition to drill I gave weapon training instruction on the No. 4 Lee Enfield rifle, the .303 Bren gun, the Thompson sub-machine gun, the Mills 36 grenade and bayonet fighting; and we used to go to Whitburn Ranges for live firing.

The colour sergeant in my company was an old DLI soldier

who was an absolute animal. I used to be involved in organizing Saturday night dances in the village hall, which meant the recruits had to move out all the beds and any other barrack room furniture before the dance, and then clean up afterwards before putting everything back before they could go to bed. Naturally they didn't like all the extra work, while the colour sergeant hated it as it disrupted his normal routine.

The food was poor at that time, but it was already in short supply as it was the early days of the War. We spent most of our pay in the village shops and pubs as there was no Naafi or canteen. Many of the recruits were in their mid-twenties and so were used to drinking in pubs and smoking.

We were short of clothing and equipment and did not have personal weapons at that stage of the War. All weapons were pooled and drawn out by squads for training. At the time of Dunkirk some of us NCOs went to Durham station to meet men of the BEF returning from Dunkirk. There we took their personal weapons and ammunition off them – those of them who still carried them – and gave them leave passes and railway warrants to go home. I remember they were tired but cheerful and defiant, although some were still a bit shattered by their experiences. It only increased my desire to 'do my bit' against Germany.

At about this time I was promoted to corporal, and a month later I was given accelerated promotion to (lance) sergeant, which at $18^1/_2$ made me the youngest sergeant in the Army. By now I was developing a good drill square voice – so much so that one day, while I was taking a squad of recruits on drill in Catherine Street near the church hall

As a young Sergeant in the DLI in 1939. 39 pattern battle dress with no insignia other than the lanyard and sergeant's stripes.

As a young Sergeant in 1939 in 39 pattern battle dress –
practical but not smart. Holding an unknown baby!

where they were billetted, the wife of one of the miners came storming out and hit me over the head with a frying pan, saying, 'You rotten bugger, treating them lads like that!'

Miss Peggy Achilles, pronounced 'Atchels', the girl who subsequently became my wife, lived at 10 Catherine Street – fortunately her mother was not the lady who hit me over the head with her frying pan. Her father was a miner in the local pit, and was an old soldier in the DLI having won the DCM in the First World War. Peggy and I first met at one of the Saturday night dances in the village hall, and after a few months she agreed to marry me. Although I used to keep in touch with my family by letter – we had no telephone at home in those days – and told them of my impending marriage, they were unable to afford the cost of travel to Willington, and so the only guests at our wedding, which took place in the village church, were my wife's family and a few army friends. On our wedding night, my parents-in-law gave us their front bedroom, but we were woken in the early hours by a tapping noise on the window – it was the 'knocker-up', the man who went round the houses with a long cane which had a stone tied to one end to wake miners for the early shift.

My new bride and I continued to stay at 10 Catherine Street after our wedding, living on my pay which by then included marriage allowance of 10/- a week.

While I was in Woking I had applied to join the newly formed airborne forces, and much to my surprise I was called forward for parachute training at Hardwick, near Chesterfield, where there was a hutted camp. For obvious reasons my wife did not want me to go, but I was young, there was a war on and this seemed to offer the sort of opportunities I was looking for. Little did I know how much I was to dislike parachuting!

The training at Hardwick was extremely tough and included instruction on specialist weapons, close combat and basic parachute drills – but the emphasis was on FITNESS. Everyone on the course was a trained soldier, but some nevertheless failed and were returned to their units (RTU'd). Towards the end of the six-week course we did our first balloon jumps, which I always found to be a most nerve-racking experience, worse than jumping from an aircraft. There is no slipstream – you just drop straight down in virtual silence. Even as a reluctant parachutist, I have always disliked balloon jumps the most!

There was little time to relax and go out at Hardwick as the working hours were long and hard, and we were always exhausted at the end of the day. There was one very attractive girl who was employed in the orderly room, and who everyone fancied. But all hopes were dashed when a certain Lieutenant Farrar-Hockley arrived to do his training – years later I met Pat again at a cocktail party at 1 Para. By then she was Mrs Farrar-Hockley, he was the commander of 16 Para Brigade and I was the QM/MTO of 1 Para.

One of the tests at Hardwick was 'milling', when we went in the ring with someone else of a similar height and build, with 8oz training gloves, and boxed until one of us dropped. There were few rules or niceties about 'milling', but fortunately for me I was already experienced in the ring, and knew how to move round it and defend myself.

Once we had passed our basic training for airborne forces

A candle – there but for the grace of God . . .

we were posted to an RAF hutted camp at Ringway, Manchester for advanced parachute training. During our eight weeks there, and in order to pass out, we did a further eight balloon jumps and eight from aircraft, being very much at the mercy of the weather and only able to jump when conditions were right. Throughout the course we retained our own capbadges, but at our 'wings' parade, taken by the course officer, we were presented with our 'red berets', wings and Quilter badge – a small badge donated by the manufacturers of our parachutes which we were able to wear on our lapels.

The RAF used to say that we were quite mad to jump out of a perfectly serviceable aircraft, and I tended to agree with them. It was always an effort for me to jump, although once

19

1942. New regiment, new kit including denison smock.

I was out of the door and my chute had opened, I found it quite exhilarating. However, once you were in the Regiment, you had to go through with it and not be seen to be scared of jumping, even though in my case it frightened the life out of me. I never looked forward to a jump, and always felt huge relief afterwards. There are those, of course, who say they love parachuting, but to my mind there is something wrong with them – it is simply not natural to leap into oblivion from a speeding aircraft. Maybe I've seen too many parachuting accidents and injuries – and deaths.

CHAPTER IV

On completion of my parachute training I was posted to the 156th Battalion of the Parachute Regiment in Melton Mowbray, Leicestershire, in early 1944. The Battalion had been formed in India in October 1941 and was made up of volunteers, with at least three years' service, from regular British Army battalions which were out there at the time. Now part of 4 Para Brigade, commanded by Brigadier Shan Hackett, it had just come home after service in North Africa and Sicily, and although very experienced, badly needed reinforcements to bring it up to its established strength of about 700 all ranks.

I was now a colour sergeant and was posted as CQMS to C Coy, under Major Geoffrey Powell MC, in the stables of Newport Lodge, Melton Mowbray. Having been formed in India the Battalion had done its parachute training at Chaklala in India, and once again Urdu was part of our everyday language. I heard hair-raising stories of jumping from Vickers Valencias and Hudson doors. The Valencia pilot sat in an open cockpit with leather gloves and headgear, and there were several nasty accidents caused by poor

'Ringing the bell' – a Whitley bomber converted for parachuting with a hole in the bottom of the fuselage.

equipment made by the Indian Army Ordnance Corps until Group Captain Maurice Newnham from Ringway visited the Army Jump School at Chaklala and a number of improvements were made. Eventually, the Battalion converted to C47s – Dakotas.

As the Battalion had been part of the new Army Air Corps or airborne forces since its formation in India, the CO, Lieutenant Colonel Sir Richard Des Voeux, and the RSM, WOI Denis Gay, both of the Grenadier Guards, insisted that all ranks should wear the new-style red beret, with Para wings on the sleeve, instead of the old-style bush hat.

By this stage of the War the Allies were advancing rapidly

across France, into Belgium and Holland, and we were repeatedly briefed for sixteen different operations, all of which were cancelled, sometimes at the last minute. It was a frustrating time being held back in England, knowing that all the action was taking place in Europe. Everyone was raring to go and security was supposed to be extremely tight. Nevertheless, one man, Lance Corporal Prince managed to escape from the guard room, break into the Naafi and steal some cigarettes and other items, before getting back into the guard room undetected – a perfect alibi! He was never found out and later jumped with us at Arnhem.

Finally, we were briefed for Operation Market Garden – the airborne landings to secure the three bridges over the rivers ahead of the advancing 2nd Army. We had about two weeks to prepare for the operation, during which we learnt that the Battalion's initial role was to hold part of the perimeter to the north of Arnhem 'for a few days'. Morale at these briefings was very high and we were all confident of success – we had been waiting around long enough. Little did we know that 9th SS Panzer Division was 'resting' in the area.

1st Parachute Brigade went in on Day 1 with the primary task of securing and holding the bridge over the Lower Rhine at Arnhem. But the Brigade was dropped too far from the bridge and although 2 Para managed to reach it first, the German reaction was swift. Bad weather and faulty signals equipment contributed to the problems. Back in England we heard only bad news of the first day's drops and of the high rate of casualties, which merely served to make us apprehensive, although we were helped on our way by local

156 Parachute Battalion, 1944. Lieutenant Colonel Sir W.R. Des Voeux Bt. with the warrant officers and sergeants a few weeks before Arnhem. Author: second from left, second row.

civilians in Melton Mowbray who seemed to know what was going on and turned out to cheer us as we left the stables for the aerodrome.

The next day, 17 September, was our turn. As we flew over the Channel I can remember seeing through the open doors great numbers of Dakotas all around us, and as we came in to the DZ I can remember there was a great deal of smoke from heathland fires started, no doubt, by signal flares and bursting mortar bombs and shells. As we dropped from the aircraft at about 600 feet I realized that we were being fired at by the Germans on the ground. Although I could not make out any enemy figures, I could clearly hear the crack of passing rounds and could see that men were being hit around me, hanging limply in their harnesses. We discovered later that we had lost about 100 men in the air and on the ground during the drop.

The situation was pretty chaotic as we tried to assemble at the company RV – this is always the time when things can go seriously wrong following a massed airborne assault. But the Company Sergeant Major (CSM), Bill Sykes, rallied the company with flares and blasts on his whistle. All the time there was a lot of swirling smoke around us, small arms fire and incoming enemy mortar and artillery rounds. I managed to get hold of a horse and cart which had been abandoned by its Dutch owner, and we loaded everyone's small packs (containing their 24-hour ration packs, spare ammunition, eating utensils, washing and shaving kit, personal clothing etc.) onto it, and set off with the company towards Wolfhezen. Eventually we were forced to split up into smaller parties and in the confusion I had to abandon the horse and cart as we had to move tactically – when I met up with Major Powell later he was unhappy to learn that we had lost all of our small packs, but blamed himself for giving the order in the first place; all I had to offer him was a small tin of margarine which we shared with relish.There was a lot of sniper fire, initially from trees and, as we got nearer to Oosterbeek, from gardens and houses, much of which was directed at officers and NCOs who could be distinguished by their badges of rank, map cases and binoculars round their necks, plus the fact that they were the ones directing operations wherever the action was. Because of this Major Powell later gave the order for all officers and NCOs to remove their badges of rank and whenever possible keep their maps in their pockets and their binoculars inside their smocks.

Although the situation was very confused at this time, Major Powell still managed to retain some control and held the occasional orders ('O') group, in spite of the constant German sniping and Spandau fire, backed up by their artillery and mortars, including 'moaning minnies', their eight-barrelled medium mortars. We watched the first supply drop come in – the sky seemed to fill with Dakotas but as the Germans still held the intended DZ and communications were so bad, the RAF dropped their loads into the middle of the enemy positions. We yelled and waved to attract the pilots' attention but of course it was no good – they could never see us, intent as they were in dropping their loads and getting away from the murderous anti-aircraft and small arms fire coming up at them. For us it was desperately frustrating and heartbreaking to watch, particularly as the pilots and their crews had stuck to their task so bravely. I witnessed the last moments of a Dakota which had been badly hit but which the pilot, Flight Lieutenant Lord, managed to keep flying until his load of parachutists had left the plane. He crashed and was killed but was subsequently awarded a posthumous VC.

By now I had a group of stragglers with me as I had started off at the rear of the company. We managed to get down in a hollow where there were 100 or more men including the Brigade Commander, Brigadier Shan Hackett. Realizing we were more or less surrounded, he gave the order to Major Powell to move the company on to Oosterbeek, and so we all got up and raced forward, firing as we went. More men went down but we got through the German lines.

I was more concerned for the safety of the men with me, than for myself, and of course for the wounded, many of whom we had to leave behind to become prisoners of war. It was a desperate time and we were getting very hungry.

As we reached the outskirts of Oosterbeek everything was quiet with the enemy no longer in evidence other than some mortar fire. The local Dutch were hiding in cellars or anywhere else that was safe, but we saw a few of them who were very friendly. Unfortunately they had very little food too so were unable to give us any, although we did manage to get a few cigarettes.

When we got to the Hartenstein, a large, prominent building set in its own grounds with hard tennis courts, we sorted ourselves out and slept on the grass for two or three hours just opposite the hotel. Any captured Germans were put in the tennis courts where they were as vulnerable to

Arnhem 1944. Dressing station outside the Hartenstein Hotel.
Note lack of insignia on the uniform of the man on the right,
also the first pattern Para helmet held by the man with his back
to the camera.

their own mortar and artillery fire as we were. I almost felt
sorry for them as there was no cover for them at all.

Although we had one small resupply we were told all the
time to conserve our ammunition which by now was
running low. As most of the firing had been at long range,
we were especially low on rifle and Bren ammunition, but
still had plenty for the Stens which we were never short of
as the Germans also used 9mm. When we did discover six
parachute resupply canisters we found that they only
contained 6-pounder anti-tank rounds and red berets!

Those left in the company were ordered to clear some of

the streets around the hotel and form part of the now much-reduced perimeter. In the nightmare days and nights that followed it was easy to become disorientated from lack of sleep and food, and the constant dangers posed by street-fighting; time meant very little. We were lucky if we had an hour's sleep in twenty-four. Without our small packs containing our 24-hour rations, and with no resupply, we were forced to live off what we could scavenge or scrounge – mostly this consisted of a few apples supplemented by cabbage storks from the gardens. This had a curious effect on us a few days later when all our body hair started to fall out!

Sub-units were mixed up and as a NCO I took command of whoever was with and around me. With communications being so poor messages were sent by runner, many of whom got shot and killed or wounded en route. There seemed to be no contact with 2nd Army south of the river as the 68 sets would not function without their crystals which had not arrived with the sets. The 38 sets worked rather better on the brigade net and we were also able to talk to 2 Para on the bridge.

On one occasion I went round the company perimeter and found a trench surrounded by broken clocks which the occupant had collected from neighbouring houses. I have no idea how he had intended to get them out, however a German sniper had spotted them and had picked them off one by one leaving our man shaking with rage and swearing profoundly at the bottom of his trench having been fired at every time he had made an attempt to retrieve a clock.

I was surprised how hyped up I was in spite of being so

short of sleep and food. I also remember noticing that the morale of the men, including the wounded, seemed to be remarkably high regardless of our worsening plight.

At such close quarters the fighting could be very unpleasant and we quickly learnt not to show ourselves in doorways or windows for fear of being instantly sniped, sometimes from as close as twenty yards. I was forced on one occasion to kill a German with my rifle and bayonet – he was coming at me similarly armed, so it was either him or me, but I was a bit quicker than him; perhaps my experience in the boxing ring helped me. I hated doing it and still think of the incident today. I also remember shooting a sniper out of a tree with my rifle, and when I looked at the fallen body it was that of a young woman of no more than sixteen.

I had another close encounter when I walked around a corner of a building – only to come almost face to face with a German armed with a Luger. As it happened, I was carrying a loaded 9mm Browning pistol – but we just stood and looked at each other before both ducking out of sight. Curiously enough I saw the same face two or three years later, after the War, in a bar in Amman, Jordan where there were Germans working for the oil companies. We recognized each other but both left immediately without introducing ourselves.

One of our biggest problems was dealing with the enemy's Tiger tanks, which could destroy a house with six rounds. If you were in a house being fired at by one of them you had to move down to the ground floor as the upper stories were demolished, and then escape via the back door before the

Sniper near the Hartenstein Hotel – a young girl belonging to a Luftwaffe Flak Artillery unit.

house was flattened. Sometimes the Germans were clever and had the back of a building covered by snipers or a machine-gun. Very often tanks would work their way down a street without supporting infantry which made it easier for us to stop them. Although our 6-pounders were very thin on the ground, we did have PIATs, a hand-held light anti-tank grenade launcher which could at least disable them. Once when I saw a Tiger tank in an adjoining street, I called up a PIAT and took it off the man carrying it as I had been well trained in its use. Working my way round to the side of the monster, risking being picked off by a sniper, I managed to hit it with a single shot in its tracks. As with everything else, we were short of PIAT ammunition so I did not stay to check on the crew of the tank – by now we had developed a great respect for the Germans' ability to fight.

We spent six nightmarish days and nights in the ghastly confusion of Oosterbeek. The weather throughout was typical for late September – misty, wet and unpleasant. The only consolation was that the Germans suffered the same as we did. But we were being slowly squeezed in towards the Hartenstein Hotel by the constant enemy pressure on us. Unlike us, they had armour and heavy weapons, food, ample ammunition, medical back-up and reinforcements. As the situation became more desperate and there was no news of 2nd Army relieving us, some of the comments by the men about the 'crap hats' were less than complimentary, but I never saw anyone despondent or ready to give up, and there was never any talk of pulling out.

By now the Commanding Officer had been killed, and Geoffrey Powell, who was commanding what little was left of the Battalion, received orders from the Brigade Commander that we were to withdraw across the Rhine to our south that night. Orders were passed and everyone was briefed; we checked that no one's equipment would rattle and tied pieces of blanket round our boots to deaden the sound of our steps. Everyone was hugely disappointed to be going, blaming 2nd Army for not relieving us days before as had been intended.

As darkness fell we began to thin out, making our way along strips of white tape which had been laid along the route to the river. Men from the Glider Pilot Regiment acted as guides and we had to actually pass through the German lines to get there. As we crept along in the dark and the rain

SCENES OF ARNHEM, SEPTEMBER 1944

On the road from the DZ to Oosterbeek using specially made trolleys to carry the 3-inch mortars and their ammunition – one of the few sunny days.

Anti-tank gun in action against German armour.

3-inch mortar crew firing on German positions.

Para sniper in the ruins of a house in Oosterbeek.

Captured German infantrymen with Para escort behind. Note the glum expressions on their faces.

Outside Queen Elizabeth Hospital, Oosterbeek – a Dutch nun tending our wounded.

we could hear them talking around us but there were no incidents and we got to the river unscathed. Any walking wounded went with us as long as they could guarantee that at no stage they would cry out from the pain of their wounds. It must have been about a mile and a half to the river although under the circumstances it seemed longer.

The crossing place was marked by star shells which made it obvious to the Germans that something was going on, and they shelled and mortared the area throughout the night. When we got there we found that Canadian and our own Royal Engineers had been busy bringing assault boats across to our bank, and had left them for us to handle ourselves – meanwhile they were busy making return trips with more boats, and were taking casualties themselves. Some boats had been damaged by shell and mortar fire, and it took a while before I found a serviceable one which fortunately had some paddles. The walking wounded were sent over first with the odd able-bodied man to assist them across the river, which was 150-200 yards wide at that point.

When I eventually crossed with about eight others I could just make out the far bank in the dark, partly because the Germans were shelling and mortaring it. Each man was still armed with his personal weapon but we were all down to the last few rounds of ammunition. All we knew was that there would be no reception on the home bank, and that we had to make for the town of Elst which was about two miles away. I set off with a party of about sixteen men in what I thought was the right direction and we marched through the rest of the night, all the time looking for something to eat. Although I could hear the sounds of the battle receding behind us, I was not aware of any other groups on the move near us.

Some time around dawn we heard the sound of a hydro-burner coming from the other side of some bushes, and I will never forget the look on the cook's face when he saw us emerging from the bushes – in our filthy, unshaven, hairless and dishevelled state, we must have been quite a sight. And so the first proper food we had for nearly two weeks was – bergoo (porridge)! It tasted wonderful. As our stomachs were so shrunk from lack of food, we were unable to eat much, although there was also some bread which we just took without asking. When an officer produced some rum we were all promptly sick.

That morning we were taken by DUKWs to behind the lines and given a 24-hour ration pack each before being taken on to a monastery for the night. While we were there the monks stole the boiled sweets and any other attractive items from our ration packs, but we did not care. It was such a relief to have a cigarette, something to eat and SLEEP properly for the first time in two weeks! Although we were not issued with a change of clothing until we arrived back in Melton Mowbray, morale was again very high, even though we had lost a lot of officers and men. A headcount revealed that 3 officers and 43 ORs had got safely back across the river – I was one of only two senior NCOs to make it back, the other one being a sergeant. There was no news of the situation in Arnhem or of 2nd Army at that stage – we only heard about it later when we got back to England.

The next day we were flown home in RAF transport aircraft before being ferried on to Melton Mowbray where, in spite of all the tragic events of the last two weeks, we were treated as returning heroes, although we ourselves were just glad to be out of it and able to rest. The people of Melton Mowbray gave us a special dinner in the Corn Exchange in the town, during which two of our comrades turned up minus their hair which produced a special welcome!

Curiously, our hair began to grow again as soon as we ate normal food again.

I was able to send a telegram to my wife to let her know I was back and was quite all right, but it was a few weeks before I was able to go home on leave, when we were both over the moon to see each other again.

As the stragglers, including the Brigade Commander, continued to trickle back from Arnhem, it was time to count the cost, lick our wounds and learn by our mistakes. Brigadier Shan Hackett wrote that the operation had not gone as well as had been expected but that he would do it again. What happened at Arnhem was an epic in the annals of British military history in which the courage and endurance of the ordinary British soldier in the face of overwhelming odds can never have been surpassed. Of the 9,000 men who went in, 7,000 killed, wounded or captured did not return from the bloody chaos of Arnhem.

From the outset Market Garden had been plagued by bad planning, poor intelligence, inadequate communications, adverse weather conditions and the fact that, under the circumstances, 1st Airborne Division was tasked with taking on too much – a bridge, indeed, too far.

After the battle the Germans moved in and looted every house that was still standing in Arnhem and Oosterbeek, and every man, woman and child was driven out of the towns. There had been hundreds of civilian casualties, fifty members of the Dutch underground were shot and only 150 houses remained intact in Oosterbeek.

A memorial plaque to all those who fell in the battle was mounted in St Mary's Church, Melton by the remnants of the Battalion and we attend a memorial service there on 13 October each year.

CHAPTER V

After Arnhem 156th Para Battalion ceased to exist as an operational unit and we were used as demonstration troops and umpires on exercises as we were obviously very experienced. About 150 all ranks had eventually returned in dribs and drabs from Arnhem, but as other airborne units were desperate for reinforcements, what was left of the Battalion was amalgamated with 1 Para in Grimsthorpe, Lincolnshire where I was promoted to WOII, and became CSM of T Company, the other companies being R, S, Sp and HQ. The Battalion was reforming and was accommodated in huts.

The only good bit of leave I had during this time was three weeks soon after Arnhem when I bought a bungalow in Willington which we called 'Arnhem'. It cost about £4,500 and we had it for four years. Our first son Tony had arrived in 1940 and then my wife had our second son David in April 1945, both boys being born at home with the aid of my wife's mother and two sisters, and the midwife. When I walked down the street on leave after Arnhem, wearing my para uniform, I was feted by the locals and treated as a hero. Miners were exempted from joining up during the War and they were therefore the same men that I had known when I had been training recruits for the DLI. I never had to buy a beer for myself in a pub during that leave!

On Christmas Eve 1944 I went down to the lake near the camp to shoot a swan for the Sergeants' Mess dinner the next day. Using a silenced Sten gun I managed to bring one down, but when I went to retrieve it I discovered that I had only creased it in the head and it was still very much alive! So I had a rather unpleasant struggle to drown it in the shallow water and mud of the lake. However the Mess duly had roast swan for Christmas dinner and no questions were asked, although I would most certainly have got into trouble had I been found out.

Shortly after the War in Europe ended 1 Para was warned off to go to Denmark, and we dropped in to an airfield near Copenhagen. From there we went to Haderslev, a town on the border between Denmark and Germany, and were tasked with policing the border area and preventing the local Danish underground from maltreating or killing the thousands of Germans from the Wehrmacht, Luftwaffe and even the German Navy who were now being sent back to Germany. They just wanted to go home but of course the Danes, who had suffered under German occupation throughout most of the War, wanted to take out their hatred and frustration on them. The thousands of defeated Germans had no one to give them orders and at first we were taking their weapons off them, but as this left them without any means of defending themselves against the Danish underground, we let them keep them as they crossed the border. We also had to relieve them of anything they had

Denmark, as WOII in 1 Para, with a nice bike.

looted, plus their Danish currency, as vast quantities of money leaving the country could have affected the economy. This money was then put in sacks and taken to banks in Copenhagen where we were well received!

We also took from the Germans any horses they had with them and I gathered a large number of them in a field, but in the confusion of those immediate post-war days I quite forgot about feeding and watering them. Danish farmers took what they wanted as most forms of local transport were horse-drawn, but a lot of the animals stampeded and escaped, no doubt eventually finding good homes all around Jutland.

One day I ordered a German colonel to get off his horse, so when he refused I drew my 9mm Browning and fired a shot into the ground in front of him, which forced him to dismount, calling me a '*Schwein*'. I put the horse in the field and sent him on his way. Later I was charged by my company commander for firing the shot and ended up being court-martialled, but thankfully the charge was dropped and I was able to return to duty.

The soldiers were accommodated in school halls and community centres, and the Danes used to invited us out to their houses and farms where they entertained and generally wined and dined us. I made a firm friend in Haderslev, a banker called Per Jorganson, who spoke good English and helped as an interpreter. I used to visit him and his wife in their home, and a few years later their son came and worked in England.

A lot of the local women had cohabited with Germans, but they must have regretted doing so as the locals sought them out and shaved off their hair so that that were instantly recognizable. People would taunt them and spit at them – a few were even tarred and feathered.

As a young lance corporal in the DLI I had been looked upon as a potential bandsman and had been sent to the Army School of Music at Kneller Hall, where they had started to train me on the clarinet. However, a few days later, after I had been playing my clarinet to a tree as practice for what seemed like hours, the Director of Music had come up to me and said, 'Thomas, there's not an ounce of melody in you – go to percussion!' So they had put me on the double bass – but I had still been RTU'd after two weeks there. Nevertheless this bit of musical training came in useful in 1 Para and I helped form a small dance band, consisting of a pianist, a bass player and an accordionist – I was the MC and band leader, occasionally playing bass. We used to perform at company dances and civilian functions, for which we were each paid the equivalent of about £1.

One day I found a guitar in a truck which we had taken off the Germans. Thinking it could be useful for the dance band I 'liberated' it, but later when I tried it out I was unable to get it to play properly. As it also seemed to be on the heavy side I opened it up and found that it was stuffed full of bags of Danish coins which I handed in – although I did keep a couple of gold ones!

Whilst in Denmark we lived in uniform and never wore civilian clothes. It was quite hard to keep the men busy at times as we were not an army of occupation, but the locals looked after the soldiers well and I do not remember anyone getting bored. The War was over but most of the men in the

Battalion were regulars and were not champing at the bit to get home, although we did have a few conscripts, or national servicemen, who were quite anxious to be discharged!

When the Battalion was eventually sent back to UK I was posted to 12th (Yorks) Para Battalion as part of 5 Para Brigade which was on its way by troopship to India to start jungle training. The war with Japan had not yet ended and on completion of our training we were to be sent on to the Far East. We sailed from Greenock on the *Corfu* and seventeen days later we were landed at Bombay, from where we were taken to Kalyan Camp, a hutted transit camp, for jungle training. There we were issued with tropical jungle green clothing and equipment and had to start taking daily mepacrine as an anti-malaria precaution. However, a few days later the Japanese surrendered, so our jungle indoctrination training was cut short and we embarked on another troopship, the *Chitral*, and sailed for north-east Malaya where we were to take part in a beach landing at Morib.

Life on board a troopship in those days was particularly unpleasant for the men, who were packed in on the troop decks, some of which were below the water level. As a CSM I was a troop deck warrant officer and faired a little better as a senior NCO. But it was an effective way of getting gradually acclimatized to the tropics.

Although we had had absolutely no preparation or training for an opposed beach landing, we were briefed to expect Japanese to be there when we landed. The night before the landing, all the medicinal brandy disappeared from the medical cabinets – removed by some of the senior

NCOs who were never found out. We left the ship by climbing down scrambling nets and were taken ashore in lighters to clear the beach of any Japs. As we closed with the shore, and thinking we were close enough in, I leapt off the lighter into the sea, but being quite short I disappeared under water. I swear to this day that I just kept on running along the sea bed until I emerged in the shallows. Looking back I saw the RSM, Bill Oliver, who was a tall man, groping around in the water for me! He was greatly relieved when I called to him as he thought I was a gonner. When we reached the treeline above the beach, we came across a British sailor dressed in tropical white uniform including long shorts, sitting on a box, calmly reading what appeared to be a comic. When I asked him who the hell he was, he replied that he was Royal Navy and they'd come up by train from Singapore. So the Navy had come up by train, while the Paras had come by ship – it all seemed rather ludicrous. However, the Japs had gone and not a shot was fired. The landing had been given the name 'Operation Fiasco' – and it was!

The next day we set off marching to Kuala Lumpur, prepared to meet opposition from the Japs at any stage. By now it was the beginning of the monsoon and to us it seemed unbelievably wet – we never seemed to be dry as we were either soaked by the rain or our own sweat. At one halt I tried to get a fire of sticks going by throwing petrol on it from a jerrycan – having always taught people never to try this method. Sure enough, the jerrycan ignited and I was burnt in my face, losing my eyebrows, the fringe of my hair and the camouflage net on my helmet. The word was gleefully passed round that the sergeant major was on fire!

12th Para Battalion, Singapore, 1945. WOs and Sergeants' Mess – author fourth from right, second row (seated).

We never reached KL but were turned back without meeting any Japs and returned to Morib. There we re-embarked on the *Chitral* – much to our chagrin as the nursing sisters on board had waved goodbye to us only days before as we bravely left the ship for the beach landing – and sailed for Singapore.

We disembarked at Singapore and once again rejoined 5 Para Brigade, under Brigadier Ken Darling, tasked with acting in aid of the civil powers. The war with Japan had only just ended and Singapore was still in chaos. We were housed in bungalows near Alexandra Hospital which had once been

By the KING'S Order the name of
Colour-Sergeant (actg.) T. Thomas,
Army Air Corps,
was published in the London Gazette on
10 May, 1945
as mentioned in a Despatch for distinguished service.
I am charged to record
His Majesty's high appreciation.

Secretary of State for War

Mention in Despatches for Arnhem – 10 May 1945.

Author with RSM Bill Oliver (right) in tropical kit – Java, 1946.

the homes of British nursing sisters. On searching the gardens we came across shallow graves from which we recovered the bodies of a number of nurses who had been brutally murdered in different ways by the Japs – one had even been crucified on a door having been raped several times. It was heart-rending, but representatives of the War Graves Commission were already arriving on the island asking for the location of any graves and/or bodies.

We had no sympathy whatsoever for any Japs who were rounded up, including some very tall members of the Imperial Guard, before taking them to Changi. We also assisted in repatriating ex-POWs, but the main aim was to get Singapore back to some semblance of order, which we found we were quite good at after our time in Denmark, even helping to get some of the 'leisure' centres working again, including the Great World, the Happy World, the New World and the Old World. To entertain the local population we gave boxing and wrestling exhibitions which we rehearsed beforehand in the gym. One of our wrestlers was Private 'Black Pete' Muckle – I met him years later running a pub in Stoke-on-Trent – who went in the ring with a hood over his head which would be removed if he had been beaten, but of course he never was. I even took part, as a CSM, in one boxing demonstration. But the locals loved it all and we were very popular, proving once again that the British soldier, when he has a job to do, does it well, and is one of our finest ambassadors.

Meanwhile the war crimes tribunals had started in the Municipal Buildings near the padang. We all knew that the Japs had ill-treated our POWs and the local population extremely badly. In their eyes to surrender was the worst possible crime and so they had been brutally cruel to all Allied POWs. Volunteers were called for from our senior NCOs to be hangmen. Although I put my name on the list I was not selected, which was quite a disappointment as I would have done the job with great satisfaction, but my colour sergeant was and got extra duty pay of 2/- per day. Apparently some Japs volunteered to be executed as in their eyes they had been disgraced.

As the city gradually returned to some sort of normality, the Battalion sailed for Java and further police-keeping duties. We were the first British troops to land there and discovered that the Japs had already surrendered to local Indonesians who were treating them worse than we would have done. The freedom fighters of Achmed Sukarno were also out to kill any Dutch civilians as they fought their own war for independence.

We were continually searching the kampongs on the jungle edge with little effect, although on one occasion I nearly shot Sukarno himself when we caught a group of terrorists in one of them. Although we shot several of them, some got away in the firefight including him.

At one stage I was sleeping in a vault in one of the banks in Batavia which we were guarding against looters. Cloth was in very short supply and people were looting houses or shops and were ripping the backs off chairs just to make clothes.

As things were gradually being brought under control, there was suddenly a mutiny in 13 Para, which consisted mostly of men from Lancashire, who considered that the

Tele: EDINBURGH 34371 Ext. 5.   Ref: V/~~Air~~ ~~Gooke~~/ RelA/Corr/1

AAC, AQC & GSC RECORD OFFICE,
The Drill Hall,
East Claremont Street,
EDINBURGH, 7.

Date   28 MAY 46

To:-   4453090   C.S.M.

THOMAS.   T. - AAC.

10 CATHERINE STREET.

WILLINGTON   C° DURHAM.

Reference your application to rejoin the Colours.

The Under-Secretary of State, The War Office, has now given authority as a special case for you to rejoin the Colours for the purpose of extending your service to complete 12 years with the Colours.

Please arrange to be medically examined by the M.O. of the nearest Unit to your home: AF.B.221 for the purpose is attached. You should also sign the form where marked in pencil and return in the enclosed envelope.

When replying please give Railway Station nearest to your home in order that travel warrant may be prepared and sent you.

You will be given approximately 7 days' notice of posting instructions.

D.C.O.
for Officer i/c Records.

BMcL.

Letter of authority for extension of service – 1946.

high standard of dress imposed upon them in their particular battalion was not necessary in a virtual wartime situation. They had a point, but the mutiny lasted a couple of weeks.

I got the impression that the Dutch were poor colonialists, who preferred to look after themselves rather than care for the people whose rights they had largely taken away. It was no wonder that Sukarno and his followers wanted them to leave.

Tropical skin disease was rife among the soldiers who went around covered in gentian violet – I remember having purple ears for several days.

After about eight months in Java the Brigade eventually returned to England aboard the *Empire Windrush* via the Suez Canal, disembarking at Southampton – back to peacetime soldiering.

CHAPTER VI

In April 1946 I was posted to the Airborne Depot at Maida Barracks, Aldershot as Company Sergeant Major of HQ Company. As I was likely to be in Aldershot for some time we let our house in Willington and Peggy and the boys moved into a married quarter in Jamaica Quarters, Wellington Lines. Tony went to the local army school and I was able to ride in to the barracks on a bike.

Life at the depot was monotonous but worthwhile and I felt a definite sense of achievement in putting the recruits through their basic training. Most of those coming through the depot had joined as regulars, a few of whom had started in the Para TA battalions, and we had no conscripts or national servicemen although a few did pass through later on. As CSM of HQ Company I was responsible for drill and weapon training, but the emphasis was very much on fitness to prepare the recruits for the parachute training which would follow. By now we had been issued with rubber-soled DMS boots although the recruits still wore studded ammunition boots during their basic training.

For a time I was PMC of the Sergeants' Mess which was a good, thriving place, well used both at lunchtime and in the

Maida Barracks, 1947. WOs and Sergeants Mess. Author (on the right) is wearing the new 1946 pattern battle dress. WO II 'Busty' Bentley next to author.

evenings. One of my fellow warrant officers was Busty Bentley who had been a sergeant in 12 Para with me and was now in charge of recruit training.

From the depot I was posted to 2 Para in Talavera Barracks, to take over from Spike Davies as Drill Sergeant, under RSM Jim Aitken. Before doing so I had to go on a drill course for warrant officers at the All Arms Drill Wing at the Guards Depot, Pirbright. After the course and back in the Battalion I deliberately set out to make my reputation as a drill sergeant, knowing that I had such a good guide and mentor in Jim Aitken, who was a true disciplinarian. Whenever there were Parachute Brigade RSMs' conferences they were always run by Jim at 2 Para;

Arnhem veterans at the Cenotaph, 1947, for a special investiture.

when I was later to become an RSM myself, I often went to him for advice.

The Battalion carried out routine training both locally and occasionally away from Aldershot, including one exercise at Holmfirth on the Yorkshire Moors, near Wakefield – 'Last of the Summer Wine' country – and another in Northern Ireland when the Battalion did a drop in open boggy country known as the 'Black Bog'. Also on the exercise were men from the 15th Parachute Battalion (TA) from Scotland. I was DZ Safety Officer, one of my duties being to count the men out as they left the aircraft. As I watched a stick of Scottish soldiers coming down, one of the parachutes collapsed at about a hundred feet and the man landed head first in the bog. I raced over to see how he was and found that his head and shoulders had disappeared, so I dragged him out by his legs and wiped way the mud from his mouth and eyes. Miraculously it seemed that the man was not seriously injured, cushioned as he was by the bog, but he had to be detained in hospital for a few day for observation. His name was Private Urquhart, the same as our Divisional Commander at Arnhem, and his parents came over from Scotland to see him. I also visited him in hospital and as it is normal in the Parachute Regiment to jump again as soon as possible after a parachuting accident, he asked me if I could arrange it. I replied, 'With your luck, son, don't bother!'

As Drill Sergeant one of my duties was to liaise with the local civil and military police as Aldershot was very much a

1950. Parade receiving the Freedom of Aldershot.
1949 Battle Dress.

garrison town – 'Home of the British Army' – and had far more 'squaddies' stationed in or around it than there are today. Some of the pubs had to be put out of bounds to the men, and when the RMPs picked up anyone who was drunk and disorderly in the town they would drive them out to the training areas and dump them in the middle of nowhere to sober up and find their own way back to barracks. It was a bad time with all three battalions, 1, 2 and 3 Para, being there together, although 3 Para were always the worst. I used to go out most evenings and visit the local police station and RMP duty room to see how things were going in the town.

Each year Aldershot District had a word-of-command competition for warrant officers from units throughout the country. Mons OCTU used to run the competition on Chobham Ridges and of course the guardsmen amongst the competitors always thought they would win. They tended to be rather tall men and because of my diminutive size they looked upon me with a certain amount of disdain – I even carried my own short pace stick, specially made from billiard cues, which I still have today. However my voice was high pitched, rather than coming from the stomach, and it carried a long way – I wiped the smiles off the faces of the guardsmen when I was adjudged the winner by RSM J.C. Lord, from the RMA Sandhurst, and the other judges.

Some years later, after I had been commissioned, I used to go quite often to the the Officers' Club in Aldershot. One lunchtime Captain Bird (who had been a corporal in 2 Para when I was drill sergeant) came in and saw me in the bar.

'Is that Major Thomas?' he asked Alan, the barman.

'Yes, he uses the club every day,' was the reply.

Transjordan, 1952. Helping to train the locals.

'Oh, I remember him when he was in 2 Para – he was an absolute bastard!'

When Alan repeated the conversation to me I smiled, and was pleased for all the right reasons.

Later I went with the Battalion to the Canal Zone in Egypt on peacekeeping duties, and while there we parachuted in to Transjordan to assist the Arab Legion in the formation of a parachute brigade. We dropped about twenty miles out of Amman, and they sent their pipe band to march with us and play us in to the capital. Many of the officers and men in the Arab Legion spoke English so there was no language problem. Their commander, General Glubb Pasha was like a god to the Arabs.

While in the Canal Zone I was able to go to Bethlehem

1953. WOI – and on the seventh day God created a paratrooper.

and visit some of the ancient churches and other well-known sites from biblical times. I remember sitting in one church listening to the monks singing the Gregorian chants, reflecting on my schooldays when I was an altar boy and used to go to church every day. Brother Antonius, my teacher, had been very strict and had instilled self-discipline in me which I was to appreciate in later years, and indeed still do to this day even though I have left the Church. As I sat there in the quiet tranquillity of that holy place, I was able to say a prayer of thanks and a few Hail Marys for my life thus far, and for having been a survivor through some difficult and dangerous times.

Back in England I was promoted to WOI and posted as RSM to 12/13 Para Battalion (TA) in Pudsey, Yorkshire, probably most famous for being the home of Len Hutton (later Sir Len), who actually lived in the same road, Pudsey Lane End, as our married quarters. One of my earliest memories of being there is of the great man storming down the street to see me after our son Tony had had a scrap with his boy. We had a bit of a shouting match, but we were only two fathers sticking up for their own sons.

When I arrived in the Battalion at Thornbury Barracks I tried to apply the same standards of discipline and dress as when I was in 2 Para, but of course I was now with the TA and after a while I was obliged to slacken off a little. The handful of regulars consisted of the CO, Training Major, Adjutant, RSM (myself) and a permanent staff instructor (PSI) with each company. I suppose I took some time to getting used to being with TA soldiers after all my years of service with regular units.

A rare moment of reflection in a most eventful career.

Certificate of Transfer to Army Reserve

Date of Transfer ....

Rank and/or Appointment on Transfer ....

Cause of Transfer ....

Corps from which Transferred ....

Service with Colours on Date of Transfer .... years .... days

Place ....

Date .... Officer .... (Signature)

.... in charge .... Records

Certificate of Discharge

Date of Discharge *5th June 1957.*

Rank and/or Appointment on Discharge *Lieutenant Officer I. (R.A.)*

Cause of Discharge *Offrs Regs. Para 503(a)(i) "Offr for the purpose of being appointed to a Commission"*

Corps from which Discharged *The Parachute Regiment*

Service on (a) with Colours *18* years *145* days
Date of Discharge (b) in the Reserve .... years .... days

TOTAL SERVICE .... *18* years *145* days

Place *Berlin*

Date *9 July 1957* Officer in charge .... Records

Service with the Colours showing Transfers, if any, to other Corps

Corps	Country	From	To	Length of Service	
				Years	Days
Durham L.I.	Home	12.1.39	9.11.43	4	302
Army Air Corps	Home	10.11.43	17.9.44	/	312
"	N.W. Europe	18.9.44	29.9.44	/	12
"	Home	30.9.44	7.5.45	/	220
"	B.L.A.	8.5.45	31.5.45	/	24
"	Home	1.6.45	6.8.45	/	67
"	India	7.8.45	8.9.45	/	33
"	Malaya	9.9.45	17.12.45	/	100
"	Batavia	18.12.45	17.4.46	/	121
Parachute Regiment	Home	18.4.46	9.2.50	3	288
Durham L.I. (Para Bn)	Home	10.2.50	3.6.51	1	114
"	M.E.L.F.	4.6.51	16.5.53	1	347
"	Home	17.5.53	26.11.53	/	194
Parachute Regiment	Home	27.11.53	5.6.57	3	191

Certificate of Discharge on Commissioning, and Record of Service as an other rank.

The old 12th Battalion had come from Yorkshire, while the 13th had been from Lancashire, so there was something of a 'War of the Roses' within the Battalion, particularly in the Sergeants' Mess. I found that Yorkshiremen could be quite rude to an outsider, and sometimes their outspokenness was out of order. They were also most ungenerous when it came to putting their hand in their pocket – people talk of Scotsmen being tight with money, but Yorkshiremen take some beating! By contrast it was an absolute pleasure to cross the border into Lancashire and call on one of the companies in Bolton or Liverpool where everyone was friendly and good-natured. I always looked forward to those visits. When 12/13 Para Battalion (TA) was renamed the 4th Para Battalion (TA) there was a lot of bad feeling as people did not like losing the old title and it was seen very much as an amalgamation.

The Battalion took part in a number of exercises, some of which included parachuting. On one occasion when we dropped on Cyprus I was told that the men on the DZ had been hoping that I, the RSM, would not make it. Apparently I was not the most popular man in the Battalion!

In 1957 I was asked by my CO if I would like to take a commission. As my days in the Army would otherwise have been numbered, both Peggy and I were happy for me to accept, taking the view that I would be embarking upon a second career, and I was duly posted as MTO to 1 Para, under Lieutenant Colonel Audry, stationed in Aldershot. It is not an easy transition becoming an officer and I took some time to get used to it, finding it hard to throw off some of

Newly Commissioned as MTO 1 Para (seventh from left), outside Officers' Mess, Albubera Barracks, Aldershot.

the old habits of a senior warrant officer, particularly where discipline was concerned.

My MT Sergeant was Sergeant Ellis who I was to meet again years later when I became Station Staff Officer (SSO) in Hohne and he was again MT Sergeant, with nearly all the drivers being locally employed German civilians. I had some hard characters in that platoon and still hear from them occasionally – typically, three of them are now publicans. I remember one of them, Corporal Sara, who was a useful middleweight boxer, asking if he could have a 48-hour pass as his wife was going to have a baby. When I replied that I did not know she was pregnant as we were used to seeing the families occasionally, he said, 'That's what I want the forty-eight for, sir!' – and later she was.

I ran the Battalion Boxing Team and we were quite successful one year when we reached the army finals, only to be beaten by 10 Regiment RASC. I also kept myself busy in the Garrison Boxing Centre as a referee or judge, and sometimes as MC.

I was put in charge, too, of 16 Para Brigade Boxing Team and on one occasion took them to Dublin to box against an Irish civilian team who we beat convincingly. We went several times to box in Jersey and I got to know the boxers on the island so well that I could write up the fights for the *Jersey Times* on the flight over. We made many friends on the island, including Deryck Seymour who owned and ran the Polm Dore, a large hotel in St Helier. He even used to send over a private jet to collect the team at Hurn Airport on a Friday and return us at the end of the weekend.

From 1 Para I went as Quartermaster to 17 Para Battalion

1959. Practising my trade, Aldershot.

1 Para Officers' Mess, Ladies Guest Night (author, seated right; Captain Bill King, opposite).

(TA) in Gateshead – once more I was back among my Geordie kinsfolk. I took over as QM from Jack Hobbs, an old friend in the Regiment, while Peggy settled down again in Arnhem, our house in Willington, which she was delighted to do as she was back amongst her own family and friends again. It seemed that I had gone full circle when I remet the lady who had hit me over the head with a frying pan, but it was wonderful to be living again amongst people who spoke with the old familiar Geordie accent.

The following is the exact wording – and spelling – of a letter I received at that time from Sergeant Drinkald in the clothing store, complaining about Sergeant Fuller ('Fulla') of the MT and Jack Road ('Redes'):

Tu Keu Em.
Joorin thi past feoo wekes (cain ti thi riorginisashin) thas bean i Loti i discharjes commin in.
Noo a knaa thiss is tellin tails butt se es fulla, well sor es bin givven is nee help ittall.
AwosGanna sea thi kornil iborim butt se es em fulla sais tellum.
Athort ad betta se u forst corse wi u bein doonbradfad moast i thi tym i canna cum in ti sea ibootthings lyke this.
Jak Redes thi sayme wen a de thi lorndry o thi taylas a can niva girra vearkil a tellyi.
Sor sumtymes a just fele lyke taekin thi lott on the buss.
Yi kna sor wen a kaim inta thi yard i cupla wekes i go a sene yi kar indcarivan gona was reely upset Noin a wuddint se ya smylin faise forri lang tyme.
A kna yill mis uss up hyar athink thi kornil wil inall but divvent yay frett becos wa arl thinkin i yi, in divvent wurry iboot thi woark cos it al bene dun ifishintly (ekseptin fo thi too a menshind) butt divvent say nowt mynd orral git me heed punshed in.
well sor al hev ti cloas noo becos its dinnatyme in waa ganni hev i chynese rash ower thi burra.

Yor faythful sorvant
J Drinkald (sgt)
Keu Ems
Cloathin Stoar
Bort Tce
Gaytsid
Coonty Durimm.

P.S.
Divvent think am loosin enny woark rytin this letta cos am deein it in mee dinna ooa.

Sinsearlee
Jim.
XXXXXXXXXX

It was at this time that I was called in by my CO one day and given the desperately sad news that our son Tony had been tragically killed in a motoring accident in Cyprus. He had been commissioned through Mons OCTU into the York and Lancaster Regiment and was Assistant Adjutant in the 1st Battalion at the time of his death. Very sadly he had just been given a regular commission and had been about to marry a WRAC Captain attached to the Royal Signals in Cyprus. We flew there for his funeral and have been back to visit his grave on several occasions. Whenever friends who knew him holiday on the island they go and tend his grave, and bring back up-to-date photographs of it.

I left the 17th Para Battalion (TA) for the Parachute Battle School in Brecon and a very different life. Once again I was the Quartermaster, but I was back with regular soldiers. The school, under the command of an old friend, Lieutenant Colonel Joe Starling, ran courses for junior and senior NCOs up to the rank of sergeant. Peggy and I were in a married quarter once more and I was able to enjoy going back to my Welsh roots, for my father and his family had originated there. During the years of the depression a lot of Welsh miners went to the North-East of England to find work, becoming known as the 'Welsh Geordies'.

While I was at Brecon I was presented with my MBE by Her Majesty The Queen at Buckingham Palace, although I had known about the award some time before it was announced, when I was still with 4 Para. The Brigade Major had borrowed our Chief Clerk's typewriter as he wanted to do some confidential typing away from the prying eyes of his own staff. When he returned it our Chief Clerk found my

Further correspondence on this
subject should quote   AODO
(AWARDS)

MINISTRY OF DEFENCE (AODO)
STANMORE
MIDDLESEX

/0 June, 1967.

Sir,

1.   I am directed to inform you that Her Majesty the Queen has
been graciously pleased to approve the following award to you

To be an Ordinary Member of the Military Division

of the Most Excellent Order of the British Empire.

Authority, London Gazette dated   **10th June, 1967.**

2.   In order that the award may be entered on your duplicate
Record of Service you must report the occurrence to your unit
orderly room for the necessary action to be taken.

3.   A further communication will be addressed to you shortly
regarding the presentation of the award.

I am,   **Sir,**
Your obedient Servant,

Director of Manning (Army)

Major (Quartermaster) Thomas Thomas (452756)

The Parachute Regiment.

1713/U (T) 7/66

Official authority for the award of the MBE – 10 June 1967.

At Buckingham Palace for the investiture of my MBE.

recommendation for the MBE typed on one of the pieces of carbon paper which were with the typewriter and showed it to me!

Peggy and I, together with Tony, drove to London on the great day and left the car in Green Park so that we could walk to the Palace for the investiture. It was a wonderful moment when my turn came – the Queen asked me what I was doing at the time, and I replied that I was helping to run a parachute battle school in Brecon. When we met up again outside after the ceremony we had our photograph taken before driving back to Wales.

$\mathcal{C}$HAPTER VII

After two tours as Quartermaster, it was a big disappointment in 1967 to go to 3 Para in Aldershot, as Families Officer. It was a job I did not relish, but I took the view that someone had to do it – and it was my turn! I soon discovered that my office was a place where people expected all manner of problems to be solved, and I would find myself counselling couples over their domestic disagreements which really ought to have been settled in their own homes. But families play a big part in the modern peacetime army and I soon learned that there is more than one connotation to the expression 'keeping the peace'!

Towards the end of 1968 the Battalion was posted to Malta and I went ahead with a warrant officer and a small staff to sort out the quarters and hirings for all the families. Peggy and I were ourselves in a quarter and I soon found that local Maltese would turn up at my door offering me properties for the Army to take over as hirings. I would then find bottles of whisky or live chickens left on my doorstep as further inducement.

Some members of the Advance Party drove their cars all the way to southern Italy and then shipped them across to

Families Officer 3 Para, Malta, 1968. Well, somebody had to do it!

Malta via Sicily. One of these was Simon Brewis, the Adjutant, who had a VW Beetle. Having safely driven the many hundreds of miles there, and on his second night on the island, he successfully wrote it off within a short distance of the barracks by failing to see a concrete bollard as he was negotiating his way back to the Mess after a night out.

Soon after arriving there I was offered the job of Staff Quartermaster at the Army School of Education in Beconsfield which not only would have meant promotion to lieutenant colonel, but would also have cut short my time as Families Officer. I willingly accepted but unfortunately the posting was cancelled when the officer I would have replaced extended for a further two years.

While in Malta the Battalion went on exercises to Cyprus which would always result in a considerable increase in the workload of the Families' Office – with the husbands away, the wives would bring their problems to me. I was therefore delighted when the Battalion returned to Aldershot after about eighteen months and I received my next posting – as Station Staff Officer (SSO) in Holne, West Germany where the garrison consisted mostly of armoured regiments, while the nearby ranges were used mainly by tanks from armoured regiments throughout BAOR and also by support weapons from infantry battalions. As SSO I was really the Garrison Quartermaster, with additional responsibilities for range safety.

We drove out to Germany in my new Ford Cortina and settled in to our married quarter in Hopten Strasse, Hohne. Amongst the boxes containing our belongings was one with David's collection of German Army militaria, which he had

MINISTRY OF DEFENCE
STANMORE, Middlesex
Telephone: 01-958 6377, *ext.* 314

Please address any reply to
MINISTRY OF DEFENCE

(MS2(QM)   )

2⁴ᵗʰ October 1968

and quote: P/452756/MS2(QM)

Your reference:

Officer Commanding
3rd Bn The Parachute Regiment

<u>Major(QM) T. THOMAS, MBE (452756) PARA</u>

      Reference 'A' - MOD 161555Z OCT
               'B' - Your 180915Z OCT
               'C' - MOD 210955Z OCT

1.   We regret any inconvenience caused by our reference 'A'
and subsequent cancellation by reference 'C'.

2.   The present incumbent of the appointment of Staff QM
Army School of Education, announced his intention of retiring
in March 1969 and immediate action was taken to select his
successor.   Notification was sent to you by signal to give
maximum notice.

3.   The officer concerned subsequently changed his mind and
decided to continue serving for a further two years and will
remain in the appointment.

4.   It is requested that Major Thomas be informed of the
circumstances.

Lieutenant-General,
Military Secretary.

Copy to: RHQ PARA

PMW

*Letter cancelling the author's appointment as Staff QM at the
Army School of Education in the rank of Lieutenant Colonel.*

started to acquire when he was eleven or twelve. Part of our quarter was a very long corridor and he insisted on decorating it with weapons and items of clothing and equipment. When he started to work for me in the camp, initially as a driver, he made friends with some of the local civilians who were also employed there, and used to bring them to the house to see his collection. As word got about, he bought or was given several more Second World War items to add to it, and became very well known locally.

The foreman for my locally employed civilian staff was a man called Bruno, who I discovered was an ex-paratrooper, or *Fallshirmjäger*. He had fought in Sicily and Arnhem so we had been on opposite sides, although we now worked together. I gave him a Parachute Regiment shield with 'To an old enemy from a new friend' inscribed on it – he was so delighted with it that he used to show it to people in the local gasthauses. We still exchange Christmas cards.

Most of the administrative staff in the garrison were local civilians employed as drivers, storemen, mechanics, clerks, cleaners, groundsmen and range safety officers. Many of them were ex-service, including marines, paras and even an ex-U-boat commander. Having taught David to drive in Brecon he got his first job there as a driver; he got on very well with his fellow civilian employees and was soon able to converse in German. His workmates would very often go to him with their problems which he would then pass on to me. Later he became a storeman with the QDGs who were part of the garrison.

One of the QDG officers was Captain Mark Phillips who was engaged to Princess Anne at the time. The married officers' quarter normally allocated to the CO of 4RTR was kept empty and available for when Princess Anne used to come out to visit her fiancé. The two of them used to ride out in the early mornings onto the ranges and often strayed into the danger area. I had quite a job keeping the all-German range security police informed of their movements. Apart from preventing them from riding on the ranges when firing was in progress, we had to keep the press away which even then was not easy. Within his own regiment, Mark Phillips was very popular and well liked by the men.

One day when I was out checking the ranges, I came upon a RMP lance corporal leading a large animal – it was a llama! Apparently it had escaped from a local zoo or someone's private animal collection. We kept it in the stables and fed it for several days before the local German equivalent to the RSPCA took it away.

On another occasion I went to a local German civilian club for a drink with David. When he saw men in the club drinking schnapps with their beer he asked if he could try one. I said OK and in true German fashion he downed it in one – but hated it so much that he has never drunk spirits since then, although he still enjoys the occasional beer.

While at Hohne I made friends with a retired colonel from the German Army, Oberst von Knotts. He was a lovely old man, brought up in the Prussian way, who had fought in the First World War and was an honorary colonel in the Second World War. He was highly respected by the locals, and he used to invite David and I to his large house for a sherry, which was exactly what we got – a sherry. We both much enjoyed our visits to the home of this splendid old man, who would tell us in his gutteral English of the rights and wrongs of both wars.

We had a very good social life while we were there with regiments of the cavalry and RTR being stationed in the garrison for several years at a time. As SSO I was regarded as 'Mr Fixit' and so invitations to mess and other functions were frequent. Peggy made a number of friends and was very happy there. I bought my first Mercedes on that tour – a 220 which, being duty free, I picked up at the Mercedes factory where they showed us round and entertained us to lunch. The three of us holidayed with that car when we drove down to Italy and I took David round the Cassino battlefield.

When my time in Hohne sadly came to an end I handed over to Tom Williams, the ex-Quartermaster of 3 Para, and we headed back to Aldershot, where I was to be OC Headquarter Company at the Parachute Depot which by then had moved to Browning Barracks.

Headquarter Company at the Depot consisted of the usual administrative sub-units – MT, REME Workshops, PRI, QM's Department, Families' Office. My quarter was in Barnsley Close, Keogh Barracks, but one day I spotted my present home up for sale (at £6,500) and we duly bought our second house. The owner was a printer who lived and worked in London so the place was empty and we were able to move straight in.

In those days bugle calls were very much part of the daily routine in Browning Barracks. Every morning on muster parade a bugler would blow a different call so that all ranks would learn the various calls. Even now when I see the postman coming up my drive I can hear 'Letters from Lizzie, letters from Lousy Lou', and on the odd occasion when I have to don my dinner jacket I remember the mess call 'Officers' wives get puddens and pies, soldiers' wives get skilly'. Each bugle call had its own rhyme – sick call was 'Sixty-four, ninety-four, he'll never go sick no more: the poor bugger's dead'.

Colonel Joe Starling was Regimental Colonel in the headquarters, and the Adjutant was Captain R.A. Smith, a most untidy but likeable officer who was known as 'Gungy Roup'. He is now known as Lieutenant General Sir Rupert Smith KCB DSO OBE QGM, Colonel Commandant of the Parachute Regiment.

After their basic training in Recruit Company, the recruits went on to 'P' (Parachute) Company, still in Browning Barracks, to get them super fit before being posted to Abingdon for their parachute training.

While I was at the Depot, David worked for a while as a friend of the Parachute Regiment Museum, but moved on later as he did not agree with the way the museum was being organized.

My final posting in the Army was as Quartermaster of HQ 16 Parachute Brigade, again in Aldershot, taking over from an old friend, Joe Legge. My ultimate boss in the headquarters was Brigadier The O'Morchoe of O'Morchoe who was very keen on Irish dancing. Knowing that at the end of that tour I was to leave the Army in 1975 after $39^1/_2$ years, I started job-hunting for my third career. I wrote a lot of letters to friends and contacts, and received a lot back in reply including some from Dubai and Oman as I was quite prepared to live and work abroad. But none really came to anything and as my time as a soldier neared its end I became quite depressed at the thought of becoming a civilian.

As a quartermaster I was a member of both the Officers' and Sergeants' Messes, both of which gave me excellent farewell parties. Although Peggy was quite pleased that we would finally be settling down for good in our own home, I faced the prospect of civilian life with some trepidation.

CHAPTER VIII

After over thirty-nine years as a soldier I knew that it would take time for me to get used to being a civilian. The Army had been my life and I missed the feeling of security and camaraderie that I had taken for granted for so long. They say that 'Once a soldier, always a soldier' and it is true – although I might add 'Once a para, always a para'.

Having failed to find a job during my final few months at the Depot, I formed a limited company, 'Inter-County Seamless Guttering', together with John Epplestone, a retired ex-para lieutenant colonel. The idea had come from a former sergeant in the Regiment who became one of the employees, while John and I provided the start-up capital to get the company going and became its two directors. We purchased two vans and took on three employees, offering an on-site service to measure, cut to size and fix aluminium guttering to buildings under construction or needing replacement guttering.

We initially advertised extensively in the local press and military publications, and gradually built up what should have been a thriving business. We used the conservatory of my house as an office and I spent most of my time there on the phone. David became our salesman; he would follow up enquiries with a site visit, measure up and give a quotation for the required job. As quotations were accepted we would then task the vans on a daily basis to go out and do the work. We did not have mobile phones in those days and so David and the men had to phone in to the office from time to time throughout the day for us to maintain contact.

Apart from the initial layout for the vans, machinery and materials the business ran itself very well until we came up against non-payment of invoices by customers. One or two of these were international companys, well known in the construction industry both at home and abroad, and had used us as sub-contractors on new-build sites. We would patiently press them for payment – which they could well afford – but we soon became accustomed to hearing the same old excuses as to why the cheque was not 'in the post'. After several months of struggling to keep going, and with even our solicitors failing to get some of our largest customers to pay us what was due, we were advised to go into voluntary liquidation. Even our employees agreed that it was the best course of action when we told them, so we sold the vans and equipment and paid off anything we owed to our suppliers, having learned the hard way that there are a lot of unscrupulous people out there in the 'real' world, where it seemed that loyalty and integrity counted for nothing. Both John and I had lost a considerable sum of money.

I licked my wounds for a few months as Operations Manager for Securiplan, Kilburn, a London-based security company which provided manned security at various office and other sites around the capital. I was responsible for organizing the various shifts and for checking that they were in place and operating efficiently and alertly at all times. Often I would go round and find that staff had not even turned up for duty – many of them were Irish and as they were poorly paid they were not reliable. The management of the company were mainly ex-Guards and were disappointingly ineffectual, so as they lurched from one crisis to another I resigned with some relief.

I had always intended to have a dog – and soon after my brief excursion into the security business had ended, I had 300 of them when I applied successfully in July 1976 for the post of Administrator and Southern Area Representative for Guide Dogs for the Blind. We let our house in Mytchett and moved in to the company flat above the centre in Wokingham. Most of the training of new guide dogs took place at the centre, and the procedure then was that a new applicant would apply through their local branch for a dog, and having been interviewed, screened and eventually accepted would stay at the centre for six weeks to be matched to and train with their new dog. We would accommodate and feed the new owners, all of whom of course were blind, during this training period. I was responsible for all the administration of the centre and of these courses, for which there was quite a large staff. Once a new owner had 'passed out', he would return home with his dog where he would be visited daily by a training instructor who would assist with continuation and familiarisation training, particularly for the dog in its new surroundings.

The administration and running costs of such a large organisation are very high, and as with all charities which have no financial help from the government, the association has to rely on voluntary donations and collections. The sixty-odd branches in my Southern Region were run entirely by unpaid volunteers, mostly from private houses, as were street and other cash collections.

In October 1977 Peggy very sadly died after a long illness. I was devastated and missed her terribly as she had been the girl I had married and lived with ever since those far-off days at the beginning of the War.

1980. Old Comrades parade. 4 Bde 156 Veterans, Oakham, Leicestershire. It comes to us all.

151/156 Parachute Battalion Association reunion – Browning Barracks, Aldershot, 1984. (Colonel Geoffrey Powell, front row, fourth from left; author, front row, fourth from right).

I was very happy working for Guide Dogs for the Blind and it gave me a great deal of job satisfaction. It was always a marvellous feeling to witness the new lease of life that a guide dog would bring to a blind person, while the dog itself seemed to really enjoy doing the job for which it had been so carefully trained. But by 1985 I had reached retirement age once more although I was retained on a consultancy basis for about three days a week to oversee various building and other projects, as required.

Having heard in May 1984 that the secretary of 151/156

156 Parachute Battalion Association reunion, Melton Mowbray, Leicestershire, 1985.

Para Battalions Association, of which I was a member, had died, I had applied to replace him, and had been accepted. The President by then was Colonel (Retd) Geoffrey Powell, my old company commander from Arnhem days.

The original 151 Battalion had been formed in India in October 1941 and so our annual reunion has always been held over an October weekend, in Melton Mowbray. We normally have a dinner on the Saturday night, and a church service at St Mary's Church, where the regimental plaque is, the following morning, followed by a lunch in the local British Legion Club. About eighty old comrades attended last year, but as the numbers dwindle, at the time of writing (March) forty-five are expected this year. I finally handed over as secretary of the association in 1996.

From General Sir John Hackett.

COBERLEY MILL
CHELTENHAM
GLOUCESTERSHIRE
GL53 9NH
01242 870207

7 November 1995

Major T Thomas, MBE,
4 Ambleside Close,
Mychett,
Camberley,
Surrey, GU16 6DG.

Dear Tony,

I was very glad to have your Newsletter No 42, regarding your
highly successful reunion in Melton. It is splendid to see
that the annual renewal continues in strength.

You have a powerful interim committee and Les Lockett
(to whom I am sending a copy of this letter) is exactly the
right chap to act as secretary.

I am sure I represent a widely spread following among old
members of the units of the 4th Parachute Brigade in thanking
you for what you have done over the years to keep 151/156 club
in such vigorous order. Long may it continue.

With all good wishes,

yours ever,
John Hackett

Letter from General Sir John Hackett.

Now fully retired and living as I do with my son, David in
my house in Mytchett, I often reflect with considerable
nostalgia on my years in the Army in general, and in the
Parachute Regiment in particular.

I always disliked parachuting, right up to my last and

150th jump when members of 151/156 Association dropped as civilians in September 1991 at Arnhem, the month of the battle. I was seventy years old at the time. But, to use a modern expression, one must 'go with the flow', and so I always had to grit my teeth and get on with it.

I believe the Parachute Regiment is very special because:
– the training to become and remain a para is particularly rigorous and tough;
– it has a unique esprit de corps and camaraderie;
– the risks and excitement involved in parachuting bind everyone together;
– in 156 Battalion, in particular, we were all at Arnhem, which has kept us in touch ever since.

RSM Jim Aitken used to say, 'If you have no discipline, you have nothing,' and it is true. The difference between today's modern army and that of fifty years ago is the lack of discipline, which unfortunately does not seem to have a place in today's world – you only have to look at our schools where teachers' hands are tied behind their backs, allowing the children to do more or less what they want in the classroom. I rue the day that National Service ended. And now the recruitment of women into the Army is not only encouraged but is being positively accelerated. I have nothing against women in general – I was married to and lived with one for thirty-seven years – but in my humble opinion the Army is no place for them, and its already diminished standards of discipline will inevitably be further undermined.

The finest battalion I served in was 2 Para as it was the best disciplined, and although I have served in 1, 2 and 3, I would always consider myself ex-2 Para.

I still enjoy getting letters from members of my regimental association. Sometimes I get requests for blazer buttons or badges which I willingly buy in the Parachute Regiment shop at the Depot and send off to whoever has asked for them – it helps me keep in touch with some of the men with whom I shared the exhilaration, optimism, confusion, fear, tragedies, humour, disappointment and, yes – discipline, of Arnhem in September 1944.

I recently had one such letter from an ex-sergeant, Donald McGlynn, of 12/13 Para battalion (TA) with whom I had served in Pudsey, Yorkshire. Part of his letter reads as follows:

> Thank you so much for your Xmas card. It was the surprise of the year when that came through my letter box and I have to say, a most pleasant surprise indeed. It at once brought memories flooding back from the days of your reign at Thornbury Barracks.
>
> Your stay did a lot for us in many ways. I remember most how you raised our standards of discipline, personal turnout and certainly not least, the improvement of the upkeep of the place. Your impact on the Sergeants' Mess was quite remarkable and gave us all a great pride in the place. It was, in fact, a time of what I described as the 'Golden Years'.
>
> Perhaps your greatest contribution, Tony, was to teach us to be better soldiers and to learn something about ourselves which would be of benefit in later years.

It was good to hear that at least some of my efforts have been appreciated!